HOT RODS

FIELD GUIDE

Dain Gingerelli

AMERICAN ICONS 1930-PRESENT

INTRODUCTION

It's appropriate that the hot rod is America's automotive icon, one that the rest of the world adores, abhors, and for many years considered to be a misfit in terms of styling and engineering concept. While the Italians are known for producing cars with sleek, sexy lines, the British for their somewhat frumpy yet elegant classics, and the Japanese for building cars that boast high-tech dependability, the hot rod is different. It's a hybrid of production-line technology blended with backyard ingenuity and savvy. To be sure, it's an all-American design, born and bred for a lifestyle like no other on Earth. Indeed, America itself is a nation of mongrels. This country is comprised of outcasts from around the world who converged on a single continent to forge its raw land into the greatest

nation ever. In the process we've also created a pedigree of people like no other on our planet. The American hot rod was borne of the same substance and character.

It began years ago during the automotive world's formative years. A handful of restless young car enthusiasts with the pioneering spirit for innovation and inspiration managed to gather various discarded automotive parts to hand-build cars that they could afford and drive. From those meager beginnings came the American hot rod as we know it today.

This book isn't intended to be a textbook history of the American hot rod. Instead, it is meant to serve as a field guide that can help you understand how the hot rod, as a car design, has impacted our society in terms of automotive accomplishments. Most of the hot rod cars and trucks—and related events and rod runs—included in this book are the result of hard work by dedicated enthusiasts who were—and are—willing to invest long hours and money into a hobby that is truly an American institution. They are, in my mind, true American heroes.

This book is divided into three basic chapters, two that focus on specific model-year cars (1909—the year that Henry Ford introduced his fabled Model T—through 1935, and then 1936 through 1965, the year that Detroit auto makers finally recognized that American motorists wanted a list of options that included more than just a radio and heater), and a final chapter that deals with the American hot rod lifestyle.

As you'll discover, Hot Rods Field Guide offers quick and easy reading. Hopefully when you finish this pocket-size tome you'll have a better, and more thorough, understanding about hot rods as they relate to being America's automotive icon. I've been a hot rod fan and enthusiast since 1959 when, as a young boy, I purchased my first AMT three-in-one 1/24th-scale plastic model car kit. That was followed by my first issue of Hot Rod Magazine (my brother Alan and I went in halves on the cover price!). And the rest, as they say, is history. I've written several books and countless magazine articles on the subject, and I can honestly say that I haven't tired of the topic yet. And I hope that I never will. In the meantime I hope that you enjoy this field guide, and learn something that you didn't know before about the world's greatest car group—the American hot rod.

–Dain Gingerelli

CONTENTS

CONTENTS

CONTENTS

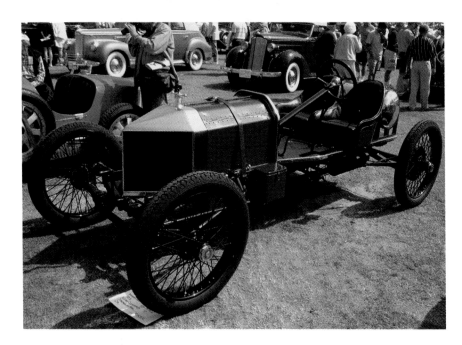

FORD MODEL T SPEEDSTER

Many hot rod historians will argue that the speedster conversion kits for Model T Fords in the early '20s represent the origins of the sport. This example, owned by Allan Clennen, showed nicely at the Newport Beach Concourse.

◆ **High-compression cylinder head**
◆ **Speedster body**
◆ **Lightweight**

MODEL T ROADSTER

Who says you can't go home again? At age 80, Gabby Garrison decided he wanted to return to his youth, so he built this Model T "soup job" that is much like the car he built back in 1933. This car has authentic Buffalo wire wheels, Essex steering, Winfield carburetor, and aluminum pistons—just like Gabby's original.

◆ **20-inch Buffalo wheels**
◆ **Winfield carburetor**
◆ **Aluminum pistons**

'32 FORD ROADSTER HIGHBOY

Art Chrisman is one of rodding's legendary figures. He built the 289-cubic-inch Ford Flathead engine that powers Joe Graffio's '32 Ford highboy. Chrisman called on some other legends for parts, too. The cam is an Iskenderian 400 Jr., ignition is Jere Jobe, and an authentic Sharp manifold holds a trio of Stromberg 97 carbs.

- ◆ **Authentic Ford Flathead V-8 parts**
- ◆ **Harwood body**
- ◆ **Custom-made exhaust**

'32 FORD DEUCE COUPE

Jimmy Houston's five-window Deuce Coupe has all the elements of a high school rod. The engine is a small-block Chevy with tri-power carburetion, the wheels are Kelsey-Hayes with wide-whitewall tires, and who can deny the classic "Four Deuces" artwork on the cowl?

- ◆ **All-steel body**
- ◆ **Original '32 frame**
- ◆ **Dropped front axle**

TRACK T RACE ROADSTER

Shortly after World War II, when Joe Graffio was still a teen-ager, he built this car to compete in the California Roadster Association race series. About 50 years later, he found the old car and bought it back to restore it as you see here. The CRA produced many racing legends, among them Troy Ruttman, who went on to win the Indianapolis 500.

- ◆ **Originally raced in 1947**
- ◆ **Originally painted by George Barris**
- ◆ **Raced by Indy drivers Joe James and Andy Linden**

'30 FORD 'PHANTOM' PHAETON

At first glance, people mistake Todd Gold's topless '30 Ford for a Phaeton. But the original Phaeton had four doors; this car has two. That's because Gold cut off the roof from a Tudor, and came up with this unique "Phantom" Phaeton. Gold owns Streamline Speed Shop in Denver, Colorado.

- ◆ '59 Cadillac taillights
- ◆ Custom 36-inch shift lever
- ◆ Body has a bullet hole

'34 FORD FIVE-WINDOW COUPE

It's sometimes difficult to part with your favorite hot rod. That explains why Joe Haska has owned his '34 Ford five-window Coupe since the early '60s. The car appeared in Street Rodder Magazine in the '70s, and has had several engines during the past 30 years. It currently relies on a Ford Flathead V-8 linked to a Chevy S-10 five-speed transmission.

◆ **All-leather interior**
◆ **Owned by custom car show promoter**
◆ **Driven "all the time" by the owner**

'25 T-BUCKET FORD ROADSTER

Even though Jack Rosen now holds the keys to this legendary '25 Ford roadster, it will forever be known as the Tommy Ivo T-bucket, in honor of the drag racer and television celebrity who built it as a hot rod in 1956. Ivo realized that the car was tall and square "like an outhouse on wheels," as he said, which accounts for the crescent-moon-shaped rear window.

- ◆ **Appeared on TV series during early '60s**
- ◆ **Drag raced during late '50s**
- ◆ **Hilborn mechanical fuel injection**

'32 FORD ROADSTER

There's nothing more rewarding than to hit the open road in a '32 Ford roadster during a crisp, clear autumn day. Jeff Nichols did just that in his car. Interestingly, this Deuce highboy was built in the '50s, then was left in a Tennessee garage for nearly 40 years before Jeff rescued it.

- ◆ Original paint job from '50s
- ◆ Original interior from '50s
- ◆ Originally built in early '50s

'32 FORD CHASSIS

It's all about the fun. Doug Bobbie was about halfway finished with his '32 Ford hot rod project when the 50th Anniversary Bonneville Nationals took place. Not wanting to miss the event, he gave his rolling body-less chassis a few additional tweaks, then headed for the Salt Flats for the celebration.

◆ **Owner collected parts for five years**
◆ **Vega cross-steer steering system**
◆ **School bus seat**

'32 FORD TUDOR HIGHBOY

Joshua Shaw was in his early 20s when he built this '32 Ford Tudor into a highboy hot rod. But he decided from the get-go to make sure his car looked as though it was built as a hot rod in the '50s. "I wanted the car to look old the first day I drove it out of the garage," he said.

- ◆ All-steel body
- ◆ Interior is not upholstered
- ◆ Built using genuine parts

'29 FORD PICKUP

Hot rodders enjoy tinkering with their cars. "I'm always working on it," said Mike Armstrong about his '29 Ford pickup. Most of his attention is given to the truck's Model B 214-cubic-inch four-cylinder engine that has an original '30s-era Cragar cylinder head. The little four-banger has an original Winfield Low End cam, Mallory dual-point ignition, and two Stromberg 81 carbs.

◆ **Dropped front axle**
◆ **Original engine and trans**
◆ **4.44:1 Columbia rear end**

'31 FORD VICTORIA

When Jim Ver Duft purchased his '31 Ford Victoria it was, as he described, "in pieces." A short time later, Gary Vahling's crew at Masterpiece Hot Rods in Denver, Colorado, had put the pieces together into the fine rod shown. The bobbed rear fenders hold '48 Ford taillights, and for power Jim selected a fuel-injected Chevrolet 350 LT-1.

- ◆ **GM 700-R4 overdrive automatic transmission**
- ◆ **Four-bar front suspension**
- ◆ **Hinged license plate swings up when parked**

'26 CHEVROLET PHAETON

Not all retro-style hot rods are Fords. Gabby Garrison selected a 1926 Chevrolet Phaeton for this project. The car was lowered, and the windshield chopped, to replicate what rodders did more than 70 years ago when Gabby built his first hot rod.

◆ **Dropped front axle**
◆ **Chevrolet four-cylinder engine**
◆ **19-inch Buffalo wheels**

AMERICAN GRAFFITI '32 FORD COUPE

Perhaps the most famous '32 Ford Coupe of all time is the American Graffiti Coupe, which starred in George Lucas's 1973 movie, "American Graffiti." The yellow coupe was built before the movie was produced. When Lucas spotted it in a shop, he knew at that moment that this was the car that would star in his low-budget but highly successful film.

- ◆ **Man-A-Fre four-carb manifold**
- ◆ **Rochester 2G carburetors**
- ◆ **Chromed headers by Johnny Franklin**

Rick Figari bought the American Graffiti Coupe in 1985 from Steve Fitch, who originally purchased it from the movie production company in the early '80s. The car has been repainted once, for the Graffiti sequel, "More American Graffiti." But for the most part the car is as original as when Paul Lamont drove it when he played the character John Milner.

◆ **Cut, or bobbed, fenders**
◆ **Prepared by Bob Hamilton for the movie**
◆ **All-black Naugahyde tuck & roll interior**

'32 FORD ROADSTER ON TRACKS

Highboy roadsters are considered the rebels of the road—and railroad! The highboy style is so named because when the fenders are removed, the body seems to be higher than normal, although it is merely perched atop the stock frame rails in the same manner as before the fenders were removed.

- ◆ '50s-era dropped front axle
- ◆ Firestone 15-inch tires
- ◆ 1940 Ford hydraulic brakes

'32 FORD FIVE-WINDOW COUPE

Dave Crouse and his crew at Custom Auto in Loveland, Colorado, restored John Walker's Deuce Coupe. The subtle Forest Green color was selected so that the car's other features—among them the authentic magnesium Halibrand wheels—would command the attention they deserve.

◆ **All-steel body**
◆ **Rare all-steel fenders**
◆ **Top chopped 3 inches**

Besides its well-proportioned chopped top, John Walker's full-fendered '32 Ford Coupe is recognized for its aluminum blisters on the hood panels. Those hand-formed pieces are for more than looks—they allow room for the Chrysler Hemi engine's wide valve covers.

◆ **Pete & Jake's ladder-bar rear suspension**
◆ **Super Bell I-beam dropped front axle**
◆ **'59 Ford F-100 pickup steering box**

'33 FORD THREE-WINDOW COUPE

The top of Doug Schaubhut's '33 Ford three-window was chopped exactly 2 1/2 inches, then the chassis was set with a 4-inch dropped front axle and de-arced leaf springs on the rear to give this car the sassy stance of a cool hot rod.

- ◆ Volvo disc brakes on all wheels
- ◆ Top chopped 2 1/2 inches
- ◆ 4-inch dropped I-beam axle

'34 FORD ROADSTER

As a drag racer in the '50s, Don Mathis learned quickly that perfection is the key to having a winning race car. That same philosophy spilled into Don's garage about 40 years later when he built this '34 Ford Roadster. The car is based on an Outlaw Performance fiberglass body and chassis combination.

◆ **Aftermarket body and chassis**
◆ **Chevrolet small-block V-8**
◆ **Convertible top**

'32 FORD ROADSTER

A word that has become popular among hot rodders today is "patina." That refers to the fading or oxidation to the paint over the years. And one roadster that boasts plenty of patina is Jeff Nichols' '32. For good reason: the car sat in a barn since 1957. Jeff gave the old hot rod a minor touch up, then put it on the road, where it belongs.

- ◆ Car appeared on a Dave Kurz painting
- ◆ Two Stromberg 97 carburetors
- ◆ Offenhauser intake manifold

'32 FORD ROADSTER
FULL-FENDERED

What's the longest you've ever owned a car? Bernie Couch bought his '32 Ford Roadster back in 1940 ("The monthly payments were about $14," he said), and he's never parted with it since. As a young rodder, he caroused with the Strokers Car Club, and raced the car numerous times at the dry lakes.

- ◆ Raced on Muroc Dry Lake in 1941
- ◆ Top speed in 1941: 97.19 mph
- ◆ 116.40 mph in '50 at El Mirage

'34 FORD COUPE

Better known as Jake, Jim Jacobs carved a name for himself in hot rod lore with this '34 Ford Coupe that he built during what amounted to a lull in his storied past. He had resigned his position as a staff writer for Rod & Custom Magazine, and had yet to join Pete Chapouris to form the parts business that became Pete & Jake's. The Coupe's most recognizable trait is the grille, which he pirated from a Ford pickup truck.

- ◆ **Purchased in '72 for $200**
- ◆ **Modified '38 Ford Pickup grille**
- ◆ **Tube front axle with four-bar suspension**

If there's one thing that Jim "Jake" Jacobs prides himself in, it's that his cars are driven. In fact, he drove his fabled '34 Ford Coupe to many NSRA Nationals, and the car has been coast to coast several times.

- ◆ **Muncie four-speed transmission**
- ◆ **First car to have Pete & Jake Vega steering**
- ◆ **Deck louvers by Gene Windfield**

'34 FORD TRUCK

This '34 Ford Pickup was built for haulin' fun. Before Fred Schlundt restored it in the late '90s, the truck had been passed along by several owners, one who chopped the top 5 inches back in the '60s. Schlundt acquired the truck from a couple in Arizona who "drove it all the time."

- ◆ **Buick 231-cubic-inch V-6 engine**
- ◆ **Super Bell 4-inch dropped tube axle**
- ◆ **Mustang steering**

Sometimes it can take a few years to complete a project. After Fred Schlundt had given his '34 Ford Pickup a coat of primer, he let it sit in the garage for three years. Then he realized that the "suede" finish actually didn't look so bad. The bed was shortened 6 inches.

◆ **'41 Chevrolet taillights**
◆ **'37 Ford pickup truck tailgate**
◆ **SAC nerf bars**

BOBTAIL '23 T-BUCKET

Long before Homer Overton built this bobtail '23 T-bucket in the mid-'90s, he was a charter member of the Shortimers Car Club, a club formed by a group of young men who happened to love hot rods, and who also happened to be serving in the U.S. Army during the Korean War. In fact, Homer was issued club plaque No. 1.

◆ Winfield "Track Grind" camshaft
◆ Ford 8-inch rear end, 3.55:1 gears
◆ VW steering

'32 FORD ROADSTER

This scene could have taken place in the late '40s, when highboy roadsters ruled the roost. But actually Rob Crouse and his Deuce roadster hit the streets back in 1999. Rob built this highboy in his father's shop, Custom Auto.

- ◆ 16-inch diameter wheels front and rear
- ◆ Windshield chopped 2 inches
- ◆ Reversed eye-springs to lower car

'29 FORD PICKUP STRETCHED

Chuck DeHaras went to one of the top hot rod shops in the country—So Cal Speed Shop—to have this stretch-cab Model A built. The original Model A frame rails were stretched 10 inches, and John Crambia and Steve Davis did most of the sheet metal work to stretch the body. The truck is powered by a classic 364-cubic-inch "Nailhead" Buick engine.

- ◆ **One-inch stretch between firewall and radiator**
- ◆ **10-inch stretch to cab**
- ◆ **Frame rails taper in at front and rear**

'29 FORD ROADSTER FULL-FENDERED

Still possessing the first hot rod you ever owned is important to many rodders, and Harold Johanson can make that boast. He bought this '29 Ford back in 1944 for $25 when he was still in high school. It has a four-cylinder with Riley overhead conversion, and was recently restored by Tom Leonardo.

- ◆ **Model B (1932) transmission**
- ◆ **16-inch Firestone wheels (adjustable spokes)**
- ◆ **'39 Lincoln hydraulic brakes**

'29 FORD ROADSTER

Low and lean best describe Jim Tuggle's '29 Ford Roadster, built by Custom Auto Restorations of Loveland, Colorado. There's plenty to notice about the car beyond its wild Dodge Viper Red paint, too. The aluminum hood was meticulously formed by hand, and the staggered louvers in the sides are strategically positioned. The V-shaped windshield was hand-built; all work by Custom Auto in Loveland, Colorado.

◆ **Model T rear spring**
◆ **Dashboard hand-formed**
◆ **Hand-formed aluminum hood**

'29 FORD ROADSTER PICKUP

As curator for the NHRA Hot Rod Museum in Pomona, California, and a hot rod author and historian in his own right, Greg Sharp appreciates historical cars. Interestingly enough, his '29 Ford Roadster Pickup can be included in that heading. It was originally built in 1962 by Dave Marasco of the Bay Area Roadster Club, and pinstriped by hot rod author and historian Andy Southard. The Pickup has been featured in several hot rod magazines.

- ◆ **Entered in 1971 Grand National Roadster Show**
- ◆ **Pinstripes by Andy Southard**
- ◆ **1955 Chevrolet 265-cubic-inch V-8**

'29 FORD ROADSTER
FULL-FENDERED

One of the more popular hot rod events on the calendar is the L.A. Roadster's Show, held every Father's Day weekend at the Pomona Fairgrounds in California. It was there in 1990 that Paul Wiener treated himself to a Father's Day present when he purchased this smoothie Model A. It has an all-steel Brookville body, and is powered by a late-model Chevy 350 IROC V-8.

◆ **Body finished in "smoothie" look**
◆ **Chevrolet II tilt-steering column**
◆ **Thrush mufflers**

BOBTAIL '29 FORD ROADSTER

Practically every year, George Poteet has a reputable hot rod shop build him a show-quality car. This bobtail modified roadster though, originated from Poteet's own garage in Memphis, Tennessee. The body, built by Old Union Car Co., is based on a '28 roadster pickup cab spliced to a '30 Phaeton rear section. Billy Tunnell finished the interior, and Gary Williams built the feisty Ford V-6 engine.

- ◆ **Model A transverse rear spring**
- ◆ **Mullins aluminum steering box**
- ◆ **Ford 9-inch rear end**

'29 FORD TUDOR FULL-FENDERED

Talk about your one-man band! Russ Wilkes not only owns Just Dreamin' rod shop in Golden, Colorado, he does all the fabrication work and assembly himself for customer cars. Naturally, he did all the work to his '29 Model A Tudor, including the upholstery. He and his wife Debbie drive the car to all events. It's also fast, as evidenced by the sedan's quarter-mile times of 12 seconds at 100 mph.

◆ Chopped top
◆ American five-spoke Torq-Thrust wheels
◆ Car is driven daily

'29 FORD ROADSTER PICKUP

There's something indescribably fun about a '29 Ford Roadster Pickup when it's built into a hot rod. Jim Siegmund will be among the first to agree. As a long-time member of the Four Ever Four car club, Jim and his son Nathaniel built this car in their garage, relying on various local shops to help fulfill the project.

- ◆ **12-volt GM alternator**
- ◆ **Brassworks radiator**
- ◆ **Bed shortened 8 inches**

'29 FORD ROADSTER FULL-FENDERED

Sometimes less is more. That's the approach that Jim Richardson took when he built his full-fendered Model A Roadster. Beneath the near-stock body is a beefed-up chassis that cradles an over-bored Model B Ford four-cylinder engine. The 216-cubic-inch engine has an Iskenderian cam, Mallory Unilite ignition, two Stromberg 97 carbs, and a homemade exhaust manifold.

◆ **Cragar overhead-valve conversion**
◆ **Cunningham billet steel connecting rods**
◆ **Arias Chevy 327 pistons**

'RACER BROWN' '29 FORD ROADSTER

One of the pioneer hot rod camshaft builders was Bill Brown, who marketed his speed equipment under the Racer Brown banner. When Tom Leonardo bought this '29 Ford Roadster in 1990, the deck lid sported the Racer Brown Cams logo, leading Tom to believe that at one time Brown raced this car. For the most part, the roadster remains as original as when it was built into a hot rod in the '50s.

◆ **'39 Ford rear spring**
◆ **Model A dropped axle**
◆ **'32 Ford frame**

MODEL A COUPE

Julio Hernandez has to practically fold himself in half to fit inside his chopped and channeled Model A Coupe. Julio says that the top was chopped 7 inches and the body was channeled over the boxed frame nearly 8 inches. The engine is a '53 Mercury Flathead with a Thickston high-rise manifold.

◆ **Mallory ignition**
◆ **Ford 8-inch rear end**
◆ **'40 Ford axle and brakes**

'29 FORD ROADSTER

It's sometimes hard to tell exactly when a hot rod is finished. "I'm still building this car," Mike Armstrong said. His '29 Roadster is based on a pair of boxed '32 frame rails and all-steel Brookville body. The engine is brand new, too. It's a Donovan Model D with overhead valve conversion. The aluminum-block engine is basically an improved replica of Ford's original Model A, B, and C fours.

- ◆ **All-steel reproduction Model A body**
- ◆ **Alloy reproduction 4-cylinder engine**
- ◆ **Three Stromberg 97 carbs**

'34 FORD TRUCK

Here's a tale about turning lemons into lemonade: Back in 1961, Wayne Cash bought this '34 Ford Pickup as his high school daily driver. Two years later, he crashed and damaged it enough that he had to park it in his grandmother's yard. It wasn't until 1987 that he was in a position to turn it into the sweet ride that it is today.

◆ **'50 Ford steering wheel**
◆ **All-steel body and fenders**
◆ **Driven annually to NSRA Street Rods Nats**

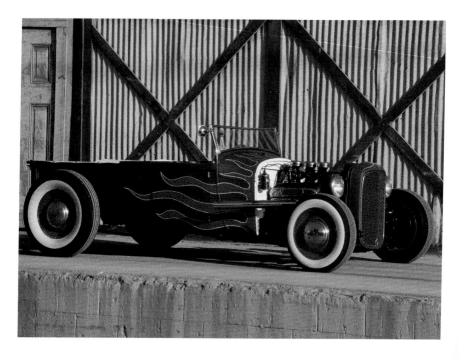

FLAMED '29 FORD ROADSTER PICKUP

All the elements for a fun ride are packed into Jonny Guilmet II's '29 Ford Roadster Pickup. We've got scallop flames on a primer finish, red steelie wheels with wide-whitewall tires, a Mexican serape blanket for upholstery, and a chopped '32 Ford radiator and grille shell to cool down the 327 small-block engine with three deuces.

- ◆ Chevrolet Powerglide automatic transmission
- ◆ Three Stromberg 97 carburetors
- ◆ Edelbrock intake manifold

'30 FORD COUPE HIGHBOY

Some projects are passed along from one person to the next before they're finished. Such was the case with this '30 Ford Coupe that John Vonderhaar completed in 1992 after trading his '49 Ford Pickup for it. The car boasts original Oldsmobile Fiesta tri-spinner wheel covers from the '50s.

♦ **'57 Oldsmobile Fiesta three-spinner wheel covers**
♦ **'32 Ford grille shell**
♦ **'39 Ford taillights**

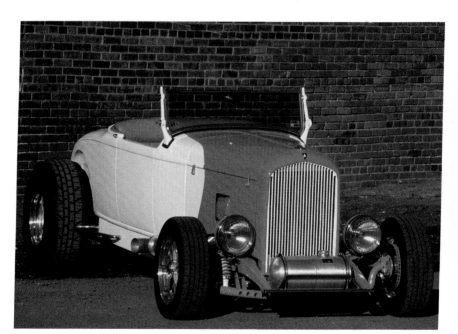

'31 PLYMOUTH ROADSTER

Few people consider modifying a '31 Plymouth Roadster into a hot rod, which is exactly why Daryl Roberts decided to undertake this project. Sticking to the Mopar theme, Roberts squeezed a 1968 Mopar 426 Hemi engine into the frame. Naturally the remainder of the drivetrain is Mopar, too; the transmission is a Torqueflite 727 and the rear end is an 8 3/4-inch Mopar Sure-Grip with 3.23:1 gears.

◆ **525 Saginaw steering box**
◆ **Four-bar front suspension inside the frame rails**
◆ **Holley 850 carburetor**

'31 FORD TUDOR

There's a lot of fun to be had with a Tudor Sedan. That's exactly what Mike and Julie Scalpo have with their '31 Ford that Mike built in four years. When it's time for rod runs, they pack the family in their Tudor and head down the highway. Besides relying on Vintage Air air conditioning to stay cool, the Scalpos look cool thanks to a 3-inch chopped roof, and fenders that have been bobbed 3 inches.

- ◆ **Rootlieb three-piece hood**
- ◆ **Digital gauges**
- ◆ **Four-bar suspension front and rear**

'29 FORD ROADSTER FULL-FENDERED

Butch Phillips is one of those guys who prefers to build his own cars. So he started with a TCI chassis—which he built—and mounted a Jim Bab's all-steel body to it (Phillips squared and detailed the body). He also rebuilt the '48 Merc Flathead engine, and restored the original Edelbrock three-pot manifold ("I had to weld a few holes shut," he said). The result is one fine-looking full-fendered Model A Roadster.

- ◆ **Shafter aluminum flywheel**
- ◆ **Vega steering box**
- ◆ **'40 Ford brakes with Buick Riviera drums**

'32 FORD COUPE

You won't find a lick of Bondo or plastic filler on this all-steel '32 Coupe built by Ron Drezek and his son Jaime. They spent more than 1,000 hours finishing the body. The cool highboy five-window is powered by a venerable Chevy 327 fed by three Rochester two-barrel carbs.

◆ **All-leather interior**
◆ **Rochester carbs on Offenhauser manifold**
◆ **Halibrand Quick-Change rear end**

'31 FORD COUPE

"Attitude" is a word often used by rodders to describe a hot rod's posture. And Craig Elderson's '31 Ford Coupe certainly has attitude. Big "meats" in the back, Moon discs on all four corners, and a 5-inch chop to the roof give this hot rod a definite attitude that will appeal to any hot rodder.

- ◆ Dropped and drilled I-beam axle
- ◆ Aldan coil-over rear shocks
- ◆ Three Rochester carburetors

'32 FORD FIVE-WINDOW COUPE

As owner of Custom Auto Restorations, Dave Crouse has restored some of the top historic hot rods in the country. Plus, he has years of experience rejuvenating Cords, Deusenbergs, and Auburns. But for his own ride, he prefers this sassy '32 Ford five-window Coupe that is rather mildly stated in appearance.

- ◆ Two-carb Weiand manifold
- ◆ 255-cubic-inch Ford Flathead V-8
- ◆ '40 Ford drums, front and rear

#25 RACE CAR

Art Chrisman is considered one of drag racing's legends. He became the first man to exceed 140 mph in the quarter-mile in his No. 25 dragster. That was in 1953, a few years after Chrisman traded a motorcycle for the car that had already made a name for itself at SCTA speed trials on the dry lake beds of Southern California.

◆ **One of the first dry lakes race cars**
◆ **One of the first drag race cars**
◆ **First to achieve 140 mph in quarter-mile**

'23 T-BUCKET ROADSTER

In 1990, a 16-year-old teen-ager named David Staller wanted his own hot rod. So he built it, scrounging and horse-trading for parts when he could. The result of his hard work is this '23 T-bucket, based on a California Custom Roadster fiberglass body. He found the Chevy 350 engine in a junkyard; then he rebuilt it himself.

◆ **Ford 8-inch rear**
◆ **Lokar shift lever**
◆ **Scott's electric radiator fan**

'32 FORD TUDOR FULL-FENDERED

Smooth is the best way to describe Woody McCormick's clean '32 Ford Tudor. The chopped sedan, named "Red Hot '32" for obvious reasons, was built by Gary Case during the late '80s. McCormick is a member of the San Bernardino, California, chapter of the Over the Hill Gang car club.

- ◆ **Smoothie look**
- ◆ **Chevy small-block V-8**
- ◆ **Turbo 350 automatic transmission**

MIX-MATCH ROADSTER

Mix-matching components is part of the fun in building a hot rod. Morgan Pennypacker must have had a lot of fun building this roadster. A '37 Dodge Pickup truck's cab—its top completely cut off—was placed on a '30 Ford frame that cradles a late-model Ford Flathead V-8. It took Pennypacker 15 days to complete the car.

◆ **Minimal amount of parts**
◆ **No upholstery**
◆ **Fine example of a rat rod**

'33 FORD ROADSTER

Creighton Hunter is considered one of drag racing's pioneers. He, along with C.J. "Pappy" Hart and Frank Stillwell, promoted what proved to be the first continuously run drag races in the country. They sanctioned their first event in July 1950 at Santa Ana Airport in Orange County, California. Hunter drives this '33 Ford Roadster today.

- ◆ **Fenderless roadster**
- ◆ **Moon discs on rear**
- ◆ **'39 Ford taillights**

'32 FORD ROADSTER

Among the landmark hot rod roadsters of the early '50s is this '32 Ford that is known among rodders today as the Joe Nitti Roadster. Originally built by a young man named Joe Nitti from East Los Angeles, the car etched its place in history when Tom Medley photographed it for the June 1950 cover of Hot Rod Magazine.

- ◆ '40 Dodge door hinges
- ◆ Originally built in 1949
- ◆ 125.18 mph at El Mirage Dry Lake, 1949

'32 FORD COUPE

Who says all hot rods are old? Gary Moline built this '32 three-window coupe using all-new components. The body is a fiberglass Downs reproduction, and the chassis—painted purple, no less—is based on components from TCI Engineering. About the only "old" component on the car is the engine, which is a smooth-running 276-cubic-inch '53 Ford Flathead.

- ◆ **Ford top-loader four-speed transmission**
- ◆ **Jeep shift lever**
- ◆ **Black all-leather interior**

A hot rod's stance is critical to how it looks. As you can see by the angle of the road, Gary Moline's '32 sits low in the front, slightly raised in the rear. This stance sometimes is referred to as the "Dago" look, in reference to the dropped front axles that Bill "Axle" Stewart built in his San Diego shop back in the '50s.

- ◆ **Vega steering box**
- ◆ **4-inch dropped I-beam front axle**
- ◆ **TCI four-bar suspension**

'34 FORD FIVE-WINDOW COUPE

The Bonneville Salt Flats is considered sacred ground among hot rodders who take their speed seriously. Dave Leuthe's '34 Ford five-window Coupe certainly makes the salt look inviting. The front bumper is an authentic '37 DeSoto component, a favorite bolt-on item among rodders throughout the years.

- ◆ **Mustang II rack and pinion steering**
- ◆ **Mustang II dropped spindles**
- ◆ **Mustang II front disc brakes**

On the surface, Dave Leuthe's '34 Ford has the makings of a retro-style hot rod. But underneath, you'll find modern running gear, including a Chevy 350 V-8, Turbo 400 automatic transmission, Mustang II independent front suspension and a venerable Ford 9-inch rear end.

◆ **Chevy ram horn exhaust manifolds**
◆ **'49 Ford dashboard knobs**
◆ **Coil-over rear shocks**

'32 FORD ROADSTER

Rob Crouse was 25 years old when he built this Roadster. And from the get-go, he set out to build a traditional-style car that evoked the spirit of rodding's early days. He scored a bull's eye, too. The highboy has a 247-cubic-inch Ford Flathead with an Isky 400 Jr. cam, Edelbrock Super two-carb manifold, and '37 Lincoln Zephyr transmission.

◆ **Traditional highboy styling**
◆ **"Big/Little" Ford wheels**
◆ **Louvers on top hood panels**

'36 FORD ROADSTER

Among Ford's most classic designs is the 1936 model. Ted Fisher realized this, and searched hard to locate a '36 roadster for his hot rod project. There was another motivational factor to his selection: His father had a similar '36 Ford Roadster for his hot rod in 1956.

◆ **Dropped front axle**
◆ **Ford Flathead V-8 engine**
◆ **Working convertible top**

There's nothing better for a hot rodder than to be sitting in his roadster with its top down. Ted Fisher enjoys the view from the seat of his '36 Ford during the NSRA Street Rod Nationals in Louisville, Kentucky. Believe it or not, this project began as a rusted hulk of a body that Ted restored.

- ◆ **Rumble seat**
- ◆ **Gooseneck shift lever**
- ◆ **All-leather interior**

'40 FORD COUPE

A few years after Jim DeLorenzo modified his '40 Ford Deluxe Coupe, he got married and had a family. Hot rods were no longer a priority so, in 1965, he built an airtight concrete garage for the '40 and literally entombed it for about 20 years. In the process, he helped preserve a part of American hot rod history.

- ◆ Chevrolet 283 V-8 engine
- ◆ Naugahyde upholstery
- ◆ Painted in 1958

'36 FORD PHAETON

If less is more, then Fred Davies' '36 Ford Phaeton has more than enough to offer the eye. Built by Masterpiece Hot Rods, the four-door drop-top is painted in Lexus Beige that's dressed with what Davies describes as chameleon flames. For power, the car has a late-model 375-cubic-inch Ford V-8.

- ◆ **200-R4 automatic transmission by Art Carr**
- ◆ **3.56:1 Positraction rear end**
- ◆ **Torsion-bar independent front suspension**

'36 FORD PICKUP UNRESTORED

What does a typical hot rod project look like before it's restored and modified? This is Tom Leonardo's '36 Ford Pickup. For years, Leonardo used the truck—as you see it—for his parts chaser. In the process, the shop mule became known as "Old Faithful," because it never broke down while chasing parts that would be used for other, and more glorious, projects.

- ◆ **Original body**
- ◆ **Original interior**
- ◆ **327-cubic-inch Chevrolet V-8**

'36 FORD PICKUP RESTORED

This is the same '36 Ford pickup truck shown on the preceding pages. Big difference, right? The old hauler was treated to new paint, an all-white interior, and, of course, a set of shiny wheels wrapped in classic wide-whitewall tires. Tom Leonardo still uses Old Faithful to chase old parts, though.

- ◆ '39 Ford steering
- ◆ '40 Ford front brakes and spindles
- ◆ 390,000 miles on same '63 Chevy rear end

'40 MERCURY

This '40 Mercury Convertible was owned by several young rodders in Michigan back in the early '50s. Among them was Jack Richardson, who dubbed the car Romango, derived by combining the name of the race horse Roman Dago. In 1984, Harry McAuliffe bought the old custom, and later restored it to the condition in which it appeared at the Detroit Autorama in 1953.

- ◆ Edelbrock two-carb manifold
- ◆ '60 Imperial 15-inch wheels
- ◆ Windshield and top chopped 4 inches

'46 FORD TUDOR

Joe Haska has about $9,000—including cost of the car—invested in his '46 Ford Tudor. A friend of his poured about $90,000 into a similar project. "Is he having 10 times as much fun as me?" Haska quipped. "I don't think so." A retired fireman in Denver, Colorado, Joe now writes for *Southern Rodder Magazine* and owns Greybeards Promotions, a company that promotes car events.

- ◆ **Original six-cylinder engine**
- ◆ **Original three-speed transmission**
- ◆ **Allstate $30 seat covers**

'37 FORD TUDOR

When '29, '32 and '40 Fords were plentiful, most rodders regarded the '37 as somewhat of an ugly duckling. Eventually, that narrow-sighted attitude subsided, and today the three-seven Ford is regarded as a very desirable car for rodding. David Julian didn't have to be told twice that this car makes for one cool rod.

- ◆ **Heidt's independent front suspension**
- ◆ **Front disc brakes**
- ◆ **Vintique wheels**

It doesn't take a rocket scientist to figure out why some Ford Tudors of the late '30s are dubbed "humpbacks." The bulging trunk lid helps define this car for rodders. This humpback '37 was built by David Julian. The personalized license plate—"N Suede"—is in reference to the car's primer finish, which is often referred to as suede.

- ◆ Tri-power Chevy 350
- ◆ Turbo 350 automatic transmission
- ◆ Ford 8-inch rear end

'37 FORD COUPE

Gary Moline has a reputation for building some of the finest retro-styled hot rods in the country. Gary built this bright red '37 Ford Coupe during the early '90s. The interior was finished in white leather and, for power, Gary installed a Ford flathead that was rebuilt by famed engine man Ken Myers of Baldwin Park, California.

- ◆ Offenhauser two-carb manifold
- ◆ '39 Ford transmission
- ◆ Ron Francis wiring kit

'36 FORD PHAETON

When Gary Vahling located this '36 Ford Phaeton, he owned and operated Masterpiece Hot Rods, one of the top rod shops in the Rocky Mountains. Even so, he didn't use his resources to change the look of the Phaeton that was originally modified by Dick Verner in the mid-'70s. "I changed the wheels and tires, and put a dropped axle on it," Vahling said, and that was about the extent of its re-fit.

- ◆ **Mor-Drop front axle**
- ◆ **'40 Ford brakes front and rear**
- ◆ **Ford 289 ohv V-8**

'38 CHEVROLET SEDAN

Driving comfort, mixed with classic hot rod lines, was what Ted Lesher aimed for when he built his '38 Chevrolet two-door sedan. The car is powered by a late-model GM 305 engine with overdrive transmission. The combination is good for nearly 30 mpg on the highway.

- ◆ **700-R4 automatic transmission**
- ◆ **Ralley wheels**
- ◆ **Whitewall radial tires**

'40 MERCURY CUSTOM

When Lyle and Sherry Penfold made the decision to customize their '40 Mercury Convertible, they chose one of the top bodymen in the country—Terry Hegman—to doll up the sheet metal. Hegman also performed, as Lyle Penfold put it, "all of the modifications to it." That included forming the aluminum top before Al Cooper trimmed it to resemble the fabled Carson tops of the '50s.

- ◆ **Cadillac 60/40 seats**
- ◆ **Digital-display instruments**
- ◆ **Remote electric doors, windows and trunk**

'41 WILLYS COUPE

If there's one street car above others that's identified with drag racing, it's the '41 Willys Coupe. Hal Rasberry knows this, which explains why his street-legal Willys looks as mean and bad as an A/Gas drag racer from the '60s.

◆ **Square-tube frame**
◆ **Weiand supercharger**
◆ **Two Holley 750 carbs**

'40 FORD TUDOR

Dave Kinnaman has always been a fan of what has become known as the Bob McCoy '40 Ford Tudor. McCoy built his flamed-Ford hot rod back in the late '50s. About 40 years later, Kinnaman decided to pay homage to the car and built this replica.

- ◆ Red and white Naugahyde upholstery
- ◆ '50s-era air cleaner
- ◆ Painted firewall white

'38 CHEVROLET TWO-DOOR

Ron Russell's '38 Chevrolet two-door has all the makings of a contemporary hot rod. Suspension is based on a Mustang II independent front and a Chassis Engineering rear, with classic American Racing Torq-Thrust wheels at all four corners. The body is finished with Chrysler Deep Amethyst two-stage paint.

- ◆ **Honda fuel door on side**
- ◆ **Briz bumpers**
- ◆ **VDO gauges**

'49 FORD AND '51 FORD

These are two similar cars, but with two entirely different styling treatments. The '49 Ford on the left is restored to original condition, while the '51 Ford on the right boasts various customizing tricks. Due to their boxy shape, the '49-'51 Fords are affectionately referred to as "shoebox Fords" by rodders.

◆ **Black car has stock spindles**
◆ **Red car has custom dropped spindles**
◆ **Custom flamed paint job**

'55 CHEVROLET

Like many hot rod owners, Gary Oliver has always had a place in his heart for his high school hot rod that he drove in 1960. That car was a red '55 Chevrolet that looked much like the car seen here. "I wanted a duplicate of my high school car," Oliver said. The clone even has white-trimmed scallops like the original.

◆ '50s-style scallop paint job
◆ Chevrolet 350 engine
◆ 3/4-race camshaft

Mild customs have always been a favorite of the street crowd. By shaving off some of the chrome trim, splashing on a cool paint job with graphics—in the case of Gary Oliver's '55 Chevy, an array of tasteful scallops—and topping the package with some flashy wheel covers, a guy can turn practically any car into a first-class cruiser.

- ◆ Celebrity autographs on dashboard
- ◆ Named "El Prado II" after Gary's first custom
- ◆ Bel Air model

'59 FORD RANCHERO

Nostalgia is the prime ingredient for Gary Moline's '59 Ford Ranchero. The Colonial White color—an authentic Ford color of the '50s—is accented by chrome-reversed wheels with '60 Ford hub caps and wrapped with wide-whitewall tires.

◆ Traction bars rear suspension
◆ Ford "top loader" four-speed transmission
◆ Spindles lowered three inches by Gene Windfield

Restoring this '59 Ford Ranchero was easy for Gary Moline—he patterned it after the one he owned back in 1959. The second iteration is powered by a Ford 390, linked to a top-loader four-speed transmission. The interior is finished in all-red leather.

- ◆ **Red all-leather interior**
- ◆ **Original '59 Ford steering wheel**
- ◆ **401 hp 390-cubic-inch engine**

'51 FORD WOODIE WAGON

When your business specializes in woodie wagons, you had better drive a woodie yourself. So Doug and Suzy Carr, owners of Wood 'n Carr in Signal Hill, California, built their '51 Ford Woodie as much for business as for pleasure.

- ◆ Stock Ford Flathead V-8
- ◆ American five-spoke Torq-Thrust wheels
- ◆ Car has appeared in numerous music videos

'53 FORD PICKUP

In the mid-'50s, Bob Jones Skyland Motors, a car dealership in Denver, Colorado, offered semi-custom Ford F-100 pickup trucks to its customers. One man who remembers those cool haulers is Jim McNaul, who duplicated a Bob Jones custom with his '53 F-100. The difference, though, is the power train. The Jones trucks were powered by Ford Flathead V-8s and later Y-blocks; Jim's half-tonner has a Cadillac 512.

- ◆ **Sig Erson camshaft**
- ◆ **'77 Chrysler front suspension**
- ◆ **Stainless steel 24-gallon gas tank**

'51 CHEVROLET COUPE

A person can have a lot of fun, at an affordable price, when it comes to building a hot rod. Bud Legg's '51 Chevrolet Businessman Coupe is an example of that. The car is lowered, chrome wheels added, and wild flames on the front clip lick back towards the doors. Too cool.

◆ '57 Chevrolet 6-cylinder engine
◆ Offenhauser manifold
◆ Three one-barrel carburetors

'56 FORD CONVERTIBLE

You'd be hard-pressed to place as much as a pack of cigarettes between Rod Roder's '56 Ford Convertible and the pavement. Air bags at all four corners account for the stance. The car retains its classic "Y-block" 292-cubic-inch engine for power.

◆ **Air bags front and rear**
◆ **Chopped windshield**
◆ **Full fender skirts**

'56 OLDSMOBILE

The commanding lines of a '56 Oldsmobile 88 Hardtop served as a great palette for Gary Moline to build a hot rod door-slammer. The Olds 88 is powered by a 371-cubic-inch J2 engine that's mated to a LaSalle four-speed transmission.

- ◆ **Traction Master traction bars**
- ◆ **Lowered 2 inches in the rear**
- ◆ **Lowered 4 inches in the front**

'55 CHEVROLET

Bad to the bone. That's the best description you can give for Karl Schuler's '55 Chevrolet that boasts the pro-street treatment. To squeeze the wide Mickey Thompson meats inside the rear quarter panels, the chassis was "tubbed." Schuler's daytime job is as a police officer.

- ◆ 6-71 GMC supercharger
- ◆ Two Holley 750 carburetors
- ◆ Three-inch diameter exhaust pipes

'57 FORD FAIRLANE 500

Talk about your daily driver. This mildly customized '57 Ford Fairlane 500 is Suzy Proche's only car. The custom treatment includes '59 Caddy bullet taillights, lakes exhaust pipes, and Olds Fiesta tri-spinner wheel covers.

◆ Original Ford "Y-block" V-8
◆ De-arched springs to lower rear
◆ '60 Ford Thunderbird steering wheel

'55 DESOTO

Three generations of builders—owner and grandson Glenn Matejel, his father Bob, and grandfather Sam—worked to put this custom '55 DeSoto on the road. The car retains its classic 330-cubic-inch Hemi engine. Sadly, Sam Matejel passed away before the project was completed. "This car is dedicated to Sam's memory," said a proud Glenn Matejel.

◆ Lowered 4-inch front and rear
◆ Shaved door handles
◆ Nosed and decked

'56 FORD SEDAN

Don't let the color combination fool you. Gary Moline's '56 Ford two-door sedan is one fast door-slammer. Powered by a Ford 390 V-8 built by Ken Myers, an engine man who cut his teeth building drag race engines in the '60s, the car can light up its M&H Racemaster cheater slicks with the drop of the foot.

- ◆ **Ford nine-inch rear end**
- ◆ **Original Ford colors**
- ◆ **Two four-barrel carburetors**

'56 CHEVROLET PANEL WAGON

What would you give for a chopped '56 Chevrolet Sedan Delivery like this? Well, Richard Freng gave away a fenderless Model A roadster. Actually, he traded the roadster to Tom Lindemann for the Jimmy wagon that sports a 5-inch chop.

- ◆ Frenched electric radio antenna
- ◆ Shaved door handles
- ◆ Nosed and decked

'57 OLDSMOBILE HARDTOP

This is certainly not your father's Oldsmobile. Jim Ross built his '57 Olds two-door hardtop with one thing in mind—having fun throughout the Rocky Mountain cruise scene. Beneath the shaved hood, you'll find the legendary J2 engine package, Oldsmobile's 371-cubic-inch engine that gulped its premium-grade gasoline through a trio of two-barrel carburetors.

◆ **Powered by fabled Olds J2 engine**
◆ **Body is nosed and decked**
◆ **Driven daily**

The junkyard is no place for Jim Ross's '57 Oldsmobile. This car has all the elements of a cool hot rod/custom. Reversed wheels with baby Moon caps dress up the wheel wells, and those Appleton replica spotlights on the cowl truly help shine the light on nostalgia fun when this car cruises into town.

◆ **Lowered front and rear**
◆ **Tucked and rolled upholstery**
◆ **Von Dutch-style pinstripes**

'56 OLDSMOBILE 88

Jonny Guilmet II claims that his '56 Olds 88 is one of the "lowest cars around with hard suspension." Translation: there are no air shocks to raise this car for driving. The fender skirts are original items, and the wheel covers are from a '57 Cadillac.

- ◆ Notched frame in rear to lower car
- ◆ Reversed eye springs and 3-inch lowering block
- ◆ Front coil springs cut 2 1/2 inches

'58 CHEVROLET BEL-AIR

"Remember When" is the theme for Danny Osburn's cool, low-riding '58 Chevrolet Bel-Air two-door hardtop. Osburn "shaved" off the door handles and rear deck emblems for the custom look. The car rides low, like a custom should.

◆ **White tucked and rolled upholstery**
◆ **Shaved door handles**
◆ **Nosed and decked**

The lakes pipes that run along the bottom kick panels on Danny Osburn's '58 Chevy got their name from hot rodding's early days. Racers on the dry lakes used a similar design for their hot rods' exhaust systems.

◆ **Bell-tip exhaust pipes**
◆ **Chevy 327-cubic-inch engine**
◆ **Competition Cams camshaft**

'55 BUICK CENTURY

Few people will deny that cars like this '55 Buick Century make the best cruisers. So Gary Moline dressed his Buick cruiser with a custom-blend metalflake from House of Kolors, then shoehorned a hefty 425-cubic-inch Buick "nailhead" V-8 under the hood. Next stop: Cruise Nite U.S.A.

- ◆ '72 Chevrolet Nova disc brakes
- ◆ Air springs front and rear
- ◆ Buick Skylark wire wheels

'58 CADILLAC ELDORADO

When it comes to the nightlife, Richard Graves feels there's nothing better than to hit the streets with his '58 Cadillac Eldorado custom. The mild custom has one feature that practically every automotive aficionado appreciates—an original stainless steel top that was original equipment on the Eldorado.

- ◆ **All-leather upholstery**
- ◆ **Halibrand-style wheels**
- ◆ **Nosed and decked**

'64 FORD GALAXY

By the mid-'60s, Detroit auto companies were producing cars with big-inch engines, much like Bill Pratt's '64 Ford Galaxy that boasts a 428 Cobra Jet engine under the hood. With street radial tires for traction, the daily driver turns quarter-mile times of 13.85 seconds at 103 mph.

◆ **Two Holley 600-cfm four-barrel carburetors**
◆ **Mallory Unilite Promaster coil**
◆ **Flo-Master mufflers with 2 1/2-inch pipes**

GRAND NATIONAL ROADSTER SHOW

The Grand National Roadster Show, held annually since 1949, is considered the granddaddy of all car shows. First held in Oakland, the show has been held in San Leandro, San Francisco, and most recently Pomona, California. This scene is from the 50th show, held at the Cow Palace.

- ◆ Oldest custom car show in the world
- ◆ America's Most Beautiful Roadster award
- ◆ Includes hot rods, customs, and motorcycles

'57 FORD CRUISING

Nothing beats spending time in a hot rod with your favorite buddies, who ride shotgun and backseat during a cruise night. This '57 Ford is cruising the main drag in town during the annual event in Paso Robles, California, that, fittingly, is called the Cruisin' Nationals.

- ◆ **Held annually on Memorial Day weekend**
- ◆ **Car show Saturday morning**
- ◆ **Good place to see classic customs**

'32 FORD ROADSTER

Although Murray Smith entered this channeled '32 Ford Roadster in the Pebble Beach Concourse, it was Jack Lentz who originally built the car 50 years ago in New England. The car is a prime example of a '50s era Northeast hot rod.

- ◆ **'51 Ford steering wheel**
- ◆ **Fenton two-carburetor manifold**
- ◆ **Louvers on hood**

AWARD-WINNING ROADSTER

Blackie Gejeian stands proudly beside the hot rod that originally won him the America's Most Beautiful Roadster award in 1955 at the Grand National Roadster Show in Oakland, California. Blackie restored the car for the Pebble Beach Concourse.

- ◆ Bobtail gas tank
- ◆ Reversed rear crossmember
- ◆ Chopped '32 Ford grille

'32 FORD ROADSTER

Bruce Meyer (left), owner of the Bob McGee '32 Ford, and Pete Chapouris, whose So Cal Speed Shop restored the famous Deuce roadster, enjoy a moment during the Pebble Beach Concourse. Typically reserved for what are considered classic cars, this and other concourses recently have come to accept hot rods, too.

- ◆ **Originally built by Bob McGee**
- ◆ **Later owned by Dick Scritchfield**
- ◆ **112.21 mph at Harpers Dry Lake, 1947**

'32 FORD ROADSTER

Hot rods are a big commodity among car collectors. Noted collector Kirk White entered this '32 Ford in the Pebble Beach Concourse. The car was originally built and owned by Ron Fiebig and W.R. Schaeneman, who raced it at El Mirage Dry Lake in 1952. The car was clocked at the Valley Timing Association meet at 128.57 mph.

- ◆ **Entered in Oakland Roadster Show, 1954**
- ◆ **Ford Flathead V-8**
- ◆ **Split windshield**

'32 FORD ROADSTER

The interior in Larry Hook's restored '32 Ford Roadster is immaculate. The car, originally built and owned by Norm Wallace in the early '50s, has its body channeled over Deuce rails. The Ford Flathead V-8 engine has a supercharger.

- ◆ **'40 Ford steering wheel**
- ◆ **Supercharged Ford Flathead V-8**
- ◆ **10 gauges on dashboard**

ALUMA COUPE

The legendary Aluma Coupe, built by Boyd Coddington in the early '90s as a concept car for Mitsubishi Motors, is inspected by the judges for the Newport Beach Concourse d'Elegance.

- ◆ **Body hand-formed aluminum**
- ◆ **Powered by Mitsubishi four-cylinder**
- ◆ **Built by Boyd Coddington**

DEACONS CAR CLUB

It's cool to be a member of a car club. Here members of the Deacons, a group of guys who call San Diego, California, home, gather around Roger Starkey's '51 Chevy Pickup truck.

- ◆ Typical "counter culture" club of today
- ◆ Members must own a hot rod
- ◆ No. 1 club rule: "There are no rules!"

JOCKO'S SCALE RACER

Toy hot rods have been an integral part of rodding. Among the favorites are tether cars, especially popular shortly before World War II. As the name suggests, the cars were tethered to a string to lap a small course for timed racing. The scale-model cars were powered by small model airplane engines.

- ◆ **Popular hobby shortly before World War II**
- ◆ **Cars raced in circles**
- ◆ **Considered collectibles today**

This scale-model tether car was built by Jocko Johnson. As a drag racer in the '60s, Johnson was among the first hot rodders to successfully apply aerodynamics to a drag race car. The tether scale-model cars that he built boast great detail. You can even see the numbers on the gauges.

- ◆ **Likeness to a real car is a must**
- ◆ **Attention to detail increases value**
- ◆ **Some cars sell for thousands of dollars**

FLATHEAD COLLECTION

After Bob Whiteside retired from the automotive industry, he decided that he was going to spend most of his time in his 1,500-square-foot shop that houses all sorts of Ford Flathead engines and components. As the sign on the wall says, "Flatheads Forever."

- ◆ Great place to hang your hat
- ◆ Ford Flathead parts are considered collectibles
- ◆ Any old, authentic part qualifies as a wall hanger

MUFFLER TIME

Stepping into the front room at Muffler Time in Oxnard, California, is like stepping back in time. You'll be greeted by dozens of old race posters and paraphernalia on the walls, and collectibles in glass cases. The collection includes race driver's suits and more rare items upstairs.

◆ **Great way to mix business with pleasure**
◆ **Displays help attract customers to shop**
◆ **Good use of old glass cabinets**

ST
HOT
MERS

RAMBLERS
GLENDALE

BENT
EIGH
LONG
BEA

LAKE
ARROWHEAD
SO.CAL.
HIPM
UNKS
66

POMONA VALLEY
TIMING ASSOCIATION

KUST
OF AME

KNIGHTS
FRESNO

TIJUANA
ZOMBIE'S

NIFT
FIFT

Car club plaques were especially popular in the late '40s and early '50s. Through time, most of the cast-aluminum plaques disappeared but, thanks to collections like this one that can be found at Muffler Time (a full-time muffler shop business!), some have survived. They make great wall hangers.

- ◆ **Plaques were hung on club members' bumpers**
- ◆ **Sometimes displayed in car's rear window**
- ◆ **Replica plaques are available today**

ENGINE TURNING

It's all about speed and great looks. This Ford hot rod boasts various speed components, but its most outstanding engine compartment feature is the engine turning on the firewall. Engine turning is a cosmetic treatment that was especially popular among high-end cars such as Cords and Auburns.

- ◆ **Engine turning was developed by aircraft industry**
- ◆ **Especially decorative on stainless steel**
- ◆ **One company, Haneline, specializes today**

ROADSTER WHEELS

The four-spoke steering wheels are referred to as "roadster wheels" by rodders. The steering wheels got their name because they were originally used in front-engine roadsters that raced on the dirt oval race tracks, as well as at Indianapolis Motor Speedway, after World War II.

◆ **Considered the true classic steering wheel**
◆ **Offer good control for driver**
◆ **Reproduction wheels are available today**

BURRITO TROPHIES

These colorful wall-hangers are made by Rey "Burrito" Fierro. Fierro constructs them out of wood, and dresses them up with small Hot Wheels cars and other toys. He then makes them available to car clubs as award trophies.

◆ **Low-cost award trophies**
◆ **Not your typical brass plaque**
◆ **Useful as home or office décor**

HOT ROD GARAGE

This is one wall of the garage that belongs to hot rod enthusiast and builder Tom Leonardo. Believe it or not, most of the old parts will eventually find a home on a hot rod that Leonardo will build for himself or restore for a customer. "I save everything," Leonardo said. "When I build a car, every part I take off it, I put up on the shelves. One day I might need it for another project."

- ◆ **A seemingly endless inventory of old parts**
- ◆ **Easy to reach during a build project**
- ◆ **Only you know where every part is**

FORD ROADSTERS

There's about 200 years of hot rod history shown parked in front of the NHRA Hot Rod Museum. At left is Ed "Isky" Iskenderian's '24 Ford, and at center is John Athan and his '29 Ford. At the far right is Tom Leonardo in the '29 Ford that he purchased years ago from its original owner and builder, Herman Leham. All three cars were built as hot rods before World War II.

◆ Typical "traditional style" hot rods
◆ All three cars built before World War II
◆ Iskenderian's car has unique overhead valve conversion

HOT ROD BUDDIES

Hot rod buddies for life. That best describes camshaft maker Ed Iskenderian (left) and John Athan (behind the wheel). Back in the late '30s Athan sold his '24 Ford Roadster to Iskenderian so he could buy this '29. As young men, they experienced many memorable events together at the dry lakes and on Los Angeles streets with their hot rods.

- ◆ Friends since high school days
- ◆ Both men still attend hot rod events
- ◆ A lot of hot rod knowledge here

A-V8 ELVIS CAR

John Athan built this A-V8—a Model A with Flathead V-8 engine—in 1939. Years later, Elvis Presley drove it in the movie, "Loving You." Consequently, Athan's car has become known as the Elvis Car. It was restored by Tom Leonardo during the late '90s.

- ◆ **Built one of the first A-V8 hot rods**
- ◆ **Instructed Elvis how to drive his hot rod**
- ◆ **Recently loaned Elvis Car to Smithsonian**

'24 FORD T ROADSTER

Ed Iskenderian has owned his Ford Roadster for more than 65 years, and the car still brings a big smile to his face. The car is on long-term loan to the NHRA Hot Rod Museum. In 1940, Iskenderian raced the '24 T to a top speed of 120 mph on the dry lakes.

- ◆ **Learned how to build cams from Ed Winfield**
- ◆ **Early cams were especially used by NASCAR drivers**
- ◆ **His Model T is in its original form, as built in 1940**

KELSEY-HAYES WHEELS

Many hot rodders strive for authenticity in the parts they select for their cars. When it comes to traditional-style wheels, many car builders agree on the spoke-laced Kelsey-Hayes wheels that were equipped on many '30s-era Fords. The Firestone 5.50x16-inch rib-treaded "tractor" tires were originally favored by early-era sprint cars.

- ◆ **Kelsey-Hayes wheels were cheap back in the '30s**
- ◆ **Authentic wheels are considered collectibles**
- ◆ **Reproduction tractor tires available today**

'32 FORD ROADSTER

The hot rod world lost track of the Joe Nitti Roadster shortly after the car was sold in the late '50s. Finally, the car surfaced again in 1994 when David Zivot located it and commissioned Dave Crouse of Custom Auto in Loveland, Colorado, to restore it, right down to the left-side radio antenna. The car earned the Bruce Meyer Preservation Award at the Grand National Roadster Show. Even the interior was restored to its original '51 condition.

- ◆ Restored hot rods are especially popular today
- ◆ Controversy: some cars are "over-restored"
- ◆ Controversy: some cars use reproduction parts

SUPERCHARGER

One surefire way to make lots of horsepower is to supercharge the engine. Superchargers—also known as blowers—essentially force more air and fuel into the engine's combustion chambers. And more air and fuel spell more horsepower. This supercharger on Hal Rasberry's '41 Willys was manufactured by Phil Weiand, who formed his high-performance company back in the early '50s.

- ◆ **Superchargers essentially pump air into the engine**
- ◆ **This is a "Roots type" blower**
- ◆ **'40 and '41 Willys Coupes were popular for drag racing**

FORD REAR ENDS

Perhaps the most desirable rear end and differential in rodding is the venerable Ford 9-inch. It is so named because its pumpkin housing measures about nine inches across. One of the most notable names associated with Ford 9-inch rear ends is Currie. These Currie 9-inch components await further machining before they are sold.

◆ **Ford introduced the 9-inch rear in 1957**
◆ **Drag racers first discovered how strong they were**
◆ **The 9-inch also offers a variety of gear ratios**

MANTARAY SHOW CAR

It's no wonder that Dean Jeffries based his Mantaray show car on the front-engine Indy roadsters of the '60s. Every year, he went to the Brickyard, where he worked into the late hours of the nights pinstriping and lettering race cars and drivers' helmets.

- ◆ **Jeffries says name is not two words, but one**
- ◆ **Jeffries hand-formed the body from aluminum**
- ◆ **Body is made from 86 pieces of aluminum**

The Mantaray began life as a pair of discarded Maserati Formula 1 Grand Prix cars that belonged to Dean Jeffries' father-in-law. He spliced the two chassis together, then hand-formed the enclosed body from aluminum. He also formed the bubble top himself. Curiously, today he says: "I wish I never put a bubble on it."

- ◆ Halibrand 15-inch magnesium race wheels
- ◆ Goodyear Blue Streak Speedway Special tires
- ◆ Steering wheel was hand-formed by Jeffries

Famous custom car builder Dean Jeffries began work on the Mantaray in 1963 in preparation for the Oakland Roadster Show of '64. He based the futuristic design on Indianapolis 500 racers that, for the most part back in '63, were front-engine cars.

- ◆ Jeffries also worked on the original Cobra project
- ◆ Jeffries painted J.C. Agajanian's race cars
- ◆ Today, Jeffries regrets putting on the bubble top

WEBER CARBS

By the early 1960s, automobile companies began offering speed equipment to the public. Ford's most notable contribution at that time bore the Cobra emblem, made famous by Carroll Shelby. This engine, with a quartet of Weber carbs, powered Dean Jeffries' famous Mantaray show car.

◆ Webers are Italian carburetors
◆ Webers were especially favored by road racers
◆ Each carburetor consists of two downdraft venturis

STEWART WARNER GAUGES

For years, hot rod builders have turned to Stewart Warner for their gauges, such as the speedometer set in this '32 Ford insert. At left is the amp meter, and at right is an old-style fuel gauge with calibration showing how much gasoline is in the tank.

◆ **Stewart Warner gauges were favored by Indy racers**
◆ **Early rodders had a mix-match of gauges**
◆ **This dash insert belongs to Bernie Couch**

'52 CHEVROLET CONVERTIBLE

To get a car's body to look perfectly smooth from any angle, most builders will strip the sheet metal bare. That's the best way to start the bodywork process. This '52 Chevrolet convertible will one day be a low-riding cruiser.

- ◆ Body men pride themselves in their work
- ◆ The less "plastic" filler used, the better
- ◆ Tools include grinders, files and sandpaper

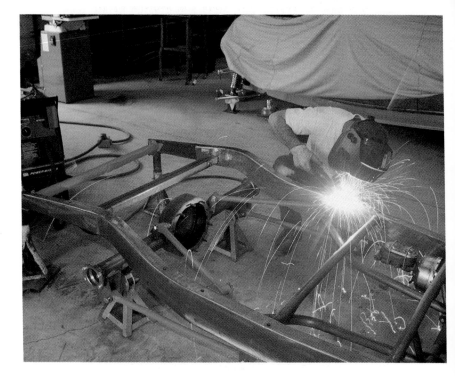

'32 FORD FRAME

Before there can be a hot rod, there must be a frame on which to attach all the other components. This '32 Ford frame is being readied for its roadster body. Often the crossmembers are strengthened or changed altogether to accommodate bigger and heavier engines, transmissions and rear ends.

◆ Crossmembers help set the width of the chassis
◆ Frame rails are "boxed" for additional strength
◆ Brake lines and wires can be routed at this time

TEX SMITH AUTOGRAPH

Hot rodding is comprised of some famous people who have lent their talents to the automotive industry as a whole. One of those legends is LeRoi "Tex" Smith, whose autograph is seen on the hood of Jeff Nichols' '32 Ford Roadster.

- ◆ Tex Smith wrote for many hot rod magazines
- ◆ Smith's XR6 won the Oakland show in '63
- ◆ Smith helped form Street Rodder Magazine in '72

TOMMY IVO T-BUCKET

The Tommy Ivo T-bucket is more than a pretty face. Its 322-cubic-inch "nailhead" Buick V-8 engine takes fuel delivery from one of Stu Hilborn's famous fuel injection systems. The combination was good for 11-second, 119-mph quarter-mile times back in '57.

◆ Tommy Ivo starred on TV's "My Little Margie" in the '50s
◆ Ivo went on to race Top Fuel dragsters in '60s and '70s
◆ Hilborn raced on the dry lakes during the '40s and '50s

BOYCE MOTOMETER
RADIATOR EMBLEM

Sometimes it's the little details that make a hot rod so interesting. And once you look beyond the Tommy Ivo T-bucket's classic lines, you can focus on some of those features. Among them is the Boyce Motometer radiator cap.

◆ **Rodders often dress their cars with special parts**
◆ **Brass plating is frequently used on T-buckets**
◆ **Norm Grabowski is credited with the first T-bucket**

ANTIQUE NATIONALS

The first weekend of June finds the staging lanes at Los Angeles County Raceway in Palmdale, California, filled with vintage hot rods and racers for the Antique Nationals. The event is sponsored by the Four Ever Fours car club, and is a favorite among many diehard rodders.

- ◆ **A car show is also held in the pits**
- ◆ **Tech inspection assures safety**
- ◆ **Competition is open to non-club members, too**

Racing against the clock or racing against time? In either case, it's non-stop action in Los Angeles County Raceway's two lanes during the annual Antique Nationals. The racing is, er, slow and furious by today's standards.

- ◆ **A full quarter-mile strip is used at the Antique Nats**
- ◆ **Racers compete head to head in their old cars**
- ◆ **Winning isn't everything here—the fun is**

DRAG SAFARI WAGON

In 1954, shortly after the NHRA (National Hot Rod Association) was formed, several of its key members created the Drag Safari. The team included Bud Coons, Chic Cannon, and Eric Rickman. The trio traveled the country to spread the word about the benefits and safety quarter-mile drag racing had to offer.

- ◆ The vehicles were recently restored by the NHRA
- ◆ Eric Rickman went on to become rodding's premier photographer
- ◆ Bud Coons was a member of the Pomona Police Department

HOT ROD REUNION

For true nostalgic fun, every year the NHRA promotes the California Hot Rod Reunion at Famosa Raceway near Bakersfield, California. Newly built cars and historic racers alike compete at this yesteryear event, while old-timers mingle in the pits to share memories.

- ◆ This event is held every autumn
- ◆ A special reunion party is held at the event, too
- ◆ The NHRA established a similar reunion in the east

HEMI UNDER GLASS

Exhibition cars were real crowd pleasers at drag races during the '60s and '70s. Among those demonstration dragsters was the Hurst-sponsored Hemi Under Glass. The car is shown making a pass at Famosa Raceway during the California Hot Rod Reunion.

- ◆ **Exhibition cars helped draw big crowds**
- ◆ **The cars did not compete for top speeds**
- ◆ **A Hemi engine powered Hemi Under Glass**

'34 FORD TRUCK

You can't go wrong with a red and white interior. Wayne Cash accented the white Naugahyde in his '34 Ford with red tucked-and-rolled panels. That classic big-rim steering wheel is from an early '50s Ford.

◆ **Naugahyde is a brand name of vinyl**
◆ **Tucked and rolled referred to the upholstery pattern**
◆ **Restored steering wheels are popular today**

PURE HELL RACER

When it came to excitement at the drags, few cars could match the Altereds that raced during the '60s and '70s. One of the legendary Altereds was Pure Hell. The car is seen making an exhibition pass at the Hot Rod Reunion.

◆ **Pure Hell often competed against Pure Heaven**
◆ **Altereds were among the hardest dragsters to drive**
◆ **Among the most famous drivers was Wild Willie Borsch**

MEMORY LANE DRAGSTER

Not all the cars at the Hot Rod Reunion are raced. Some help form the exhibit in the parking lot known as Memory Lane. This stubby front-engine rail helps spectators define the connection between street-going hot rods and early dragsters.

◆ Early rail dragsters used many original car parts
◆ Wheelbases grew longer to improve traction and control
◆ Dick Craft's "The Bug" is among the earliest dragsters

6 Months or 30,000 Miles of Going Topless

'32 ROADSTER

Andy Brizio, also known as the Rodfather, built this car with his son Roy to help celebrate the spirit of hot rodding. Andy drove the car to various hot rod events throughout the country in 1997, racking up more than 30,000 miles in six months in the cool Deuce roadster.

- ◆ **Andy Brizio's main business was producing T-shirts**
- ◆ **Brizio's T-kit car won the Oakland show in 1970**
- ◆ **Brizio's son, Roy, is among the top rod builders today**

WOODEN TOOL CHEST

Even the tool boxes were different back in the '50s and '60s. This wooden chest belonged to a member of the Smokers, a Bakersfield, California-based car club that promoted the racing at the legendary Famosa Raceway. The annual Smokers' Meet pitted all the best Top Fuel dragsters from the country in one meet.

- ◆ The NHRA banned nitro fuel for several years
- ◆ The Smokers never did
- ◆ Famosa Raceway looks much like it did 30 years ago

BRUCE MEYER TROPHY

In the interest of preserving landmark hot rods, Bruce Meyer—an established hot rod collector and enthusiast in his own right—established the Hot Rod Preservation Award. It is presented each year at the Grand National Roadster Show to a deserving restored hot rod that best represents the spirit of the sport. Fittingly, the award carries Meyer's name on it.

- ◆ Concourse d'Elegance promoters recognize hot rods, too
- ◆ Bruce Meyer has restored several other hot rods
- ◆ Authenticity is important in winning this award

'29 A-V8 ROADSTER

One of hot rodding's most outspoken enthusiasts was the late Bill Burham. He owned his '29 A-V8 Roadster for many years. Here he's seen cruising the grounds at the '95 L.A. Roadster Show.

- ◆ The first L.A. Roadster Show was held at the Hollywood Bowl
- ◆ The event's swap meet is considered one of the best
- ◆ Roadster owners are presented a commemorative mug

MUROC REUNION

It took a lot of negotiating with the U.S. military, but in 1996, the SCTA was able to promote its first speed trials event on the fabled Rogers Dry Lake (formerly Muroc Dry Lake) since 1942. Many people consider Muroc the birthplace of rodding. Today the dry lake bed forms the landing site for NASA's space shuttles, among other top secret planes.

◆ **Muroc was often the site for endurance speed records**
◆ **Early racers competed side by side at Muroc**
◆ **Chuck Yeager landed on Rogers after his Mach 1 flight**

If you squint just right, and don't pay attention to some of the cars in the background, this scene at the Muroc Reunion could have taken place in 1948 when dry lakes racing was in its prime. Although Muroc was closed to the public after World War II, racing continued at El Mirage, Harpers and Rosamond dry lakes nearby.

- ◆ **Winter rains flood the dry lake beds**
- ◆ **The lake beds drain quickly**
- ◆ **When dry, the lake bed surface feels like cement**

ROUTE 66 RENDEZVOUS

Wanna cruise the streets with your hot rod's exhaust pipes uncorked? Then venture to San Bernardino, California, every autumn for the Route 66 Rendezvous. The city reserves a couple hours during Saturday afternoon at the Rendezvous for the "symphony."

- ◆ **Route 66 was known as the Mother Road**
- ◆ **It was also known as Main Street U.S.A.**
- ◆ **The Rendezvous also has a Hall of Fame**

CARLSBAD RACEWAY

Hot rodders are known for their T-shirts that boast logos and names familiar to other rodders. These four guys share a bench in the bleachers at Carlsbad Raceway near San Diego, California. Every year racer Russ Ayres promotes what amounts to a private party—the racers and spectators must be invited in order to attend.

- ◆ **It's a party, but it's also serious racing**
- ◆ **Carlsbad Raceway was built in the early '60s**
- ◆ **Spectators can visit the pits at this event**

FORD FLATHEAD V-8

Perhaps the most distinguishable engine known to rodding is the Ford Flathead V-8. It was first produced in 1932, and discontinued after 1953 in favor of an overhead-valve design. This is an early-year Flathead, with Edelbrock heads and a four-carb intake manifold.

- ◆ Henry Ford held up production in '32 for the V-8
- ◆ Flatheads were the engine of choice for early rodders
- ◆ Slipping a Flathead V-8 into a Model A creates the A-V8

FORD MODEL T RUNABOUT

Mel Kibbee sits in his Ford Model T runabout speedster while waiting to make a run at the Antique Nationals. Companies in the '20s offered conversions like this that mounted to Ford's venerable Model T chassis to make them lightweight—and fast.

◆ **There were dozens of speedster conversions in the '20s**
◆ **Ed Winfield established himself in a Model T speedster**
◆ **Speedster-bodied T's competed on oval tracks, too**

DASHBOARD PLAQUES

The top plaque on the Holland Special racing roadster is dated 1948, and shows that J.L. McClelland raced the car. The yellow plaque commemorates McClelland racing the car 30 years later at the now-defunct Irwindale Raceway drag strip. This photo was taken at the Antique Nationals.

- ◆ **Dash plaques were common at early race events**
- ◆ **SCTA plaques are among the most coveted**
- ◆ **Every entrant was presented with a plaque**

'29 MODEL A TUDOR

If you got 'em, smoke 'em. This '29 Ford Tudor lights up its slicks on the starting line at the Antique Nationals in Palmdale, California. The car boasts some classic speed tricks, including the Moon pressure tank up front, a drilled I-beam axle, and open headers.

◆ **Slick tires were developed for traction at the drags**
◆ **Drilling parts made them lighter in weight**
◆ **Pressure fuel tanks assured immediate delivery of gas**

FLAMES ON COWL

When it comes to top speed, every hot rodder knows where to go—SCTA Speed Trials. The SCTA was originally formed in 1937 as a sanctioning organization to promote races on Southern California's fabled dry lake beds in the Mojave Desert. The wide-open spaces, and rules to govern the racers, provided a safe haven for the young drivers. Moreover, it gave legitimacy to the sport.

- ◆ **Decals have always been popular with rodders**
- ◆ **SCTA (Southern California Timing Association)**
- ◆ **The SCTA helped promote a car show in 1948**

'55 CHEVROLET 454

The heartbeat of Karl Schuler's '55 Chevy is this supercharged 454 engine that's been bored to 462 thirsty cubic inches. Feeding the legendary 6-71 GMC blower are a pair of 750-cfm (cubic feet per minute) Holley four-barrel carburetors.

- ◆ **The 6-71 GMC blower was originally for boats**
- ◆ **GMC blowers were also known as Jimmys**
- ◆ **6-71 refers to the air ratio the blower delivers**

DRAGS TROPHY

It's all for the glory. Even back in the early '50s, rodders cared about how other people perceived their cars, and so trophies were presented at car shows and races. Among the first sanctioned quarter-mile drags was the Orange County Drags in 1950, held at Santa Ana Airport.

- ◆ **Three young men promoted the first Santa Ana Drags**
- ◆ **CJ "Pappy" Hart, Creighton Hunter, and Frank Stillwell**
- ◆ **The drag strip was actually the airport runway**

RODIFICATION

Patience is often a virtue when it comes to retaining a car's original parts and components during its "rodification" period. Here seasoned rod builder Tom Leonardo hammers on a rear fender that will be used for his '36 Ford Pickup.

◆ **Many rodders do their own metal work**
◆ **Fiberglass reproduction fenders are common**
◆ **Some parts are restored using fillers such as Bondo**

MODEL A SEDAN

One of the most fun events held in Southern California is the annual River City Reliability Run. This invitation-only gathering is held in the spirit of the reliability runs of the late '40s and early '50s. The meet gets its name because promoter Mark Morton stages the event from Riverside, California.

- ◆ Traditional-style rods comprise the River City Run
- ◆ The run generally lasts 100 or so miles
- ◆ The Pasadena Reliability Run in '48 was among the first

'37 FORD TUDOR

There's something to be said about the nostalgic charm of an old Ford dashboard. Never is it more prevalent than on David Julian's '37 Ford Tudor. Most of the dash was left intact. But the billet aluminum insert and "banjo" steering wheel—not to mention that bright red paint—tell you this is no stock dashboard.

◆ First thing people look at is the car's dashboard
◆ Billet parts make it easy for anyone to customize a dash
◆ One way to dress up a dashboard is with pinstripes

HOT RODDER GARAGE

What does a hot rodder's garage contain? Besides at least one hot rod, you'll find a bunch of tools, spare parts that have been removed or are about to be installed, and maybe some speed equipment like the helmets hanging on the wall of Creighton Hunter's garage.

◆ A man's...garage...is his castle!
◆ Refrigerators are handy items in the garage, too
◆ The car on the left is an in-progress project

T-BUCKET ROADSTER

Homer Overton's T-bucket roadster is powered by Ford's "baby" Flathead, the venerable V8-60, so named because the 135-cubic-inch engine produced 60 hp. The V8-60 was introduced in 1937 as a replacement for the Model C four-cylinder. The V8-60 was kept in production until 1941, when Ford introduced its inline six-cylinder as the company's base-line economy engine.

◆ **V8-60s were often used to power midget race cars**
◆ **Cost, and minimal performance, led to its demise**
◆ **At a glance, the V8-60 looks like a full-size Flathead V-8**

AMERICAN GRAFFITI LICENSE PLATE

If you're a film fan of producer George Lucas, you know the source of his THX 138 trademark sign that appears on the credits of all of his movies. It's the American Graffiti Coupe's license plate number. As with most of the car, the yellow California tags are the originals that appeared in both movies.

◆ Much of "American Graffiti" was filmed in Petaluma, CA
◆ Look for the THX 138 logo on the credits of a Lucas film
◆ California dropped the yellow tags in the early '60s

AMERICAN GRAFFITI COUPE

Where are they now? Rick Figari still owns the American Graffiti Coupe, and often displays it at hot rod and other automotive functions. As for actor Paul Lamont, he often joins Figari and the Coupe to sign autographs and pose for pictures. This photo of Lamont sitting in the car was taken at a Viva Las Vegas event.

- ◆ **Viva Las Vegas is a popular western-states event**
- ◆ **Paul Lamont's movie career didn't take off as expected**
- ◆ **The '55 Chevy driven by Harrison Ford still exists**

'32 FORD TUDOR

Looking to give his "new" hot rod an old-time look, Joshua Shaw located this Mobil Gas emblem and Bonneville Speed Trials tag at a Midwest swap meet, then restored it before attaching it to his '32 Ford Tudor.

- ◆ **Nostalgia is especially popular among young rodders**
- ◆ **Bumper badges have been used for many decades**
- ◆ **Mobil's flying horse was a familiar fixture at races**

'32 FORD TUDOR INTERIOR

Assuming the pose you'd see in a 1950s-era hot rod magazine, young Joshua Shaw sits in his '32 Ford Tudor during the NSRA Street Rod Nationals, held annually in Louisville, Kentucky. Check out the seat mounts and shift linkage.

- ◆ Floor shifts have always been favored by rodders
- ◆ As long as it's safe, it doesn't have to look finished
- ◆ Chopped tops sometimes require new seat mounts

'32 FORD COUPE CHASSIS

Beneath a hot rod's shiny body and all the dazzling chrome-plated parts lies its chassis. This view of Gary Moline's '32 Ford Coupe before the body was set on it reveals a lot about the car. You can see the brake lines, drive train, and crossmembers that tie the frame rails together.

◆ **This is the time for the builder to tend to the detail**
◆ **At this point, the chassis is near ready for the body**
◆ **Replica chassis can speed up the project's completion**

JAGUAR REAR SUSPENSION

Back in the early '70s, rodders discovered that an independent rear suspension system pirated from a pedigree Jaguar XKE sports car worked just fine beneath one of the American-bred mongrel hot rods. This unit sits beneath Jim Ver Duft's '31 Ford Victoria.

- ◆ **Corvette independent rear suspension was popular, too**
- ◆ **The XKE's inboard brakes allowed for fatter tires**
- ◆ **Demand for IRS eventually led to aftermarket kits**

FOUR-CYLINDER FORD ENGINE

Jim Siegmund said there could be only one kind of engine for his '29 Ford—an early Ford four-banger. In this case, it was a Model C originally built by FoMoCo in '34. The 214-cubic-inch engine has a .012-inch overbore, fabled Riley four-port head (two intake valves per cylinder) with two dual-throat Weber carbs, and tube exhaust headers.

- ◆ **George Riley was an early supplier of race parts**
- ◆ **Tube exhausts can be fabricated in the shop**
- ◆ **Donovan offers an aluminum Model D four-cylinder**

ONE-SEAT DRAGSTER

Some of hot rodding's legendary pioneers once sat in this interior, among them Harry Lewis who built the one-seat modified roadster in the mid-'30s. Other owners included Jack Harvey, his brother George, then Ernie McAfee, Jack Lehman, Doug Carruthers, and LeRoy Neumayer. Finally, Art Chrisman acquired the car, and converted it into a dragster.

- ◆ Franklin steering box
- ◆ Handmade steering wheel
- ◆ Single-seater

CRUISE NIGHT

Summer fun for hot rodders all across America is accented with summer cruise nights held at local venues. Many cruise nights are sponsored by local chambers of commerce that arrange for entire city blocks to be closed to all but the hot rods. These two cars are part of the Garden Grove, California, Friday night cruise.

- ◆ **Cruise nights can help a community's economy**
- ◆ **Car clubs sponsor cruise nights, too**
- ◆ **Most cruise nights welcome cars up to the '70s**

DONUT DERELICTS

Every Saturday morning, without fail, hot rodders and car enthusiasts meet in front of the donut shop at the corner of Magnolia and Adams streets in Huntington Beach, California, to talk cars. The tradition dates back to the '70s. At some point, the rodders earned the nickname Donut Derelicts.

- ◆ **Parking space is limited for the Donut Derelicts**
- ◆ **Donut shops make great places to meet**
- ◆ **Local merchants now sell Donut Derelicts decals**

L.A. ROADSTERS

If you like hot rod roadsters, then you'll love the L.A. Roadsters Show, held every Father's Day Weekend at the fairgrounds in Pomona, California. More than 600 roadsters show up, among them the sponsoring club's member cars.

- ◆ **L.A. Roadster membership is limited to roadster owners**
- ◆ **Setup time begins Friday for the swap meet**
- ◆ **Celebrities such as Tim Allen show up, too**

ROADSTERS, PHAETONS

The Roadsters and Phaetons seen in the shade of a tree eventually spill out to the hundreds of other open-top cars parked in what amounts to the main arena at the L.A. Roadsters Show.

- ◆ **The mood is relaxed throughout the two-day event**
- ◆ **Charter members included Tex Smith and Tom McMullen**
- ◆ **Several members later helped form the NSRA**

'40 FORDS

There's a valid argument that the 1940 model year rates as the most stylish ever from Ford Motor Company. And every year the Forties Unlimited car club of Southern California sponsors a meet open to this classic. The meet is held at LaPalma Park in Anaheim, California.

- ◆ Other cars besides '40 Fords are welcome
- ◆ '40 Ford Coupes were popular as jalopy racers in the '50s
- ◆ This is a one-day event

FORTIES UNLIMITED

Vintage '40 Fords come from all parts of the country for the Forties Unlimited's annual car fest in Anaheim. There's no denying the classic, smooth, sloping rear lines of the '40 Ford Coupe.

- ◆ **Open-air car shows are popular across the country**
- ◆ **Breakfast, raffles and music define these events**
- ◆ **The stars of the show, though, are the cars**

WALLY PARKS

No book about hot rods today would be complete without a picture of Wally Parks, considered the patriarch of the sport. Wally helped form the SCTA in 1937. He served as *Hot Rod Magazine's* first "hired" editor until Ray Brock took over during the early '60s, and he was the guiding force in establishing the NHRA in 1951. He remained the consummate gentleman throughout.

- ◆ **The NHRA is a leading race sanctioning organization**
- ◆ **The SCTA still promotes dry lakes racing**
- ◆ **The SCTA also sanctions the Bonneville Nationals**

BONNEVILLE SALT FLATS

Not every run down the fabled Bonneville Salt Flats is a success, as evidenced by these parts scattered on the salt. The pin at the bottom left commemorates the Bonneville National's 50th anniversary. This photo illustrates the pebble-size salt granules that comprise the Salt Flats. Today the salt is about one to two feet thick; 50 years ago it was more than eight feet in some sections.

- ◆ **The Salt Flats are what remain of Bonneville Lake**
- ◆ **The Bureau of Land Management governs the Salt Flats**
- ◆ **A black line painted on the salt marks the race course**

Part of the Bonneville Nationals' 50th anniversary celebration in 1998 included opening the Salt Flats raceway to a fast-moving parade of street rods. They got to follow the same black stripe that the racers do when competing for a land speed record.

- ◆ **Speeds were limited to about 50 mph**
- ◆ **Land Speed Record racers must race both ways**
- ◆ **The Salt Flats are 125 miles west of Salt Lake City**

SPEED SPORT ROADSTER

Originally from Tucson, Arizona, the Speed Sport modified roadster held numerous drag racing records in the '50s. Its nitro-burning Chrysler engine was positioned behind the driver for better traction. It was restored, and later displayed at the '98 Hot Rod Reunion.

◆ **This was among the first mid-engine racers**
◆ **The Speed Sport team was especially active in the West**
◆ **The Speed Sport roadster was recently restored**

'32 HIGHBOY COUPE

It's all about speed. So Ron Drezek dressed up his highboy '32 five-window Coupe with the most recognizable thing in racing—the checkered flag. The black-and-white graphics begin at the radiator shell and hood panels, then flow across the cowl to the doors.

◆ **Graphics have always been popular**
◆ **This '32 body is finished in metal only—no plastic fillers**
◆ **Flames are perhaps the most popular graphics used**

WELDING GRILLE TEETH

It's been said that it's the journey, and not the destination, that makes rodding so much fun. And so many rod builders find as much—sometimes more—enjoyment in restoring their old cars than they do driving them! Here the teeth to an old Ford grille are meticulously welded to their original form.

- ◆ Most rod projects begin in the garage
- ◆ Too hot a flame and the metal will be ruined
- ◆ Too cool a flame and the metal won't bond at the weld

HOT ROD MUSEUM

When the NHRA Hot Rod Museum opened in 1998, hot rodders finally had a place they could call home. The museum continually rotates cars on display. So there's always something new to view when you return for another visit.

◆ **The museum is located on the Pomona Fairgrounds**
◆ **The NHRA rotates the displays on a regular basis**
◆ **The museum is open six days a week**

CHEVROLET 283 V-8

This Chevy 283 small-block V-8 is the same engine that Jim DeLorenzo swapped into his '40 Ford Deluxe Coupe in 1958. During his teen-age years, DeLorenzo drove the coupe daily. He also entered it in several custom car shows, and drag raced it at places like the now-defunct Colton Dragway.

◆ **Chevrolet introduced the small-block as a 265**
◆ **Its compact size makes it suitable for most rod projects**
◆ **The Chevy small-block also can be built for horsepower**

'40 FORD INTERIOR

Although Dave Kinnaman built his '40 Ford hot rod as a tribute to the Bob McCoy '40 Ford Tudor, he took the liberty to give the car some of his own styling cues. Among them is the interior, which is finished in bright red and white Naugahyde.

- ◆ Red is always a popular color for a hot rod
- ◆ Naugahyde looks like leather, but at a cheaper price
- ◆ Bob McCoy is better known for his hot rod art

'32 FORD PINSTRIPES

Although pinstripes were used on such classic cars as Duesenbergs, it was the American hot rod that brought the art form to a whole new level. Perhaps the most famous striper ever was Kenneth Howard, better known as Von Dutch, who inspired the style of striping shown.

◆ Horsehair brushes are used for pinstriping
◆ Most stripe jobs are applied free-hand
◆ Stripes are also used as borders between two colors

MOON DISC WHEEL COVER

Among the first hot rodders to capitalize on the hobby was Dean Moon, who developed the Moon Disc wheel covers that he made from spun aluminum. The wheel covers were originally intended for streamlining effects at the Bonneville Salt Flats and the quarter-mile drags. They became popular among the street crowd, too, as seen on Craig Elderson's '31 Ford Coupe.

◆ **Racers attach Moon Discs using sheet metal screws**
◆ **Dean Moon was a successful drag racer, too**
◆ **Moon Equip offers a variety of spun-aluminum products**

ANTI-BLESSING

A counter culture movement has gained momentum among rodders during the past 10 years. These rat-rods, so named for their rough look, gathered at Hart Park in Orange, California, for the Anti-Blessing of the Cars.

♦ **This event was in response to the Blessing of the Cars**
♦ **The cars were positioned on the open spaces of the park**
♦ **Custom car builders from the '50s often attend**

PLEXIGLASS DOME CAR

The Jetsons' car? Hardly. This extensively modified roadster sports a bubble top as a tribute to the late Ed "Big Daddy" Roth, who used many of these same styling tricks on his award-winning cars in the '60s and '70s. This tribute to Big Daddy was built by Anthony Castaneda.

- ◆ Interesting cars show up at some events
- ◆ Big Daddy was best known for the Rat Fink character
- ◆ Rat Fink T-shirts were worn by kids in the '60s

SUPER WINFIELD HEAD

One of the pioneers in the speed equipment industry was Ed Winfield, who gained fame for his camshafts and cylinder heads. This high-performance flathead was developed by Winfield in the '30s for Model A, B and C four-cylinder engines.

- ◆ Ford Fours were sometimes used in sprint race cars
- ◆ Overhead-valve conversions were popular for the Fours
- ◆ Squeezing 100 hp from a Four was considered good

MODEL A HILLCLIMB

Who says old hot rods can't still be race cars? The Model A Ford Club of America promotes hill climbing races expressly for that purpose. This modified roadster is competing at the F.A.S.T. (Ford A Speed Technology) Hillclimb that included a 6 percent grade along a 1/10th mile course.

♦ **This course was on a public street**
♦ **Racing is also open to cars other than Model A Fords**
♦ **Racers compete from a standing start**

'32 FORD ROADSTER

What does it take to upholster a "real" hot rod? Not much, really. Take a standard bench seat, wrap it with a genuine Mexican serape blanket, and you've got a first-rate upholstery job.

- ◆ The serape blanket is easy to clean
- ◆ Another popular upholstery fix is the Tijuana Tuck
- ◆ The Tijuana Tuck was from Mexico

PLEASANTON NATIONALS

Take plenty of warm California sunshine that spills across big shade trees and fresh green grass, mix in a couple thousand street rods of every color and variation, and you've got the Pleasanton Nationals that takes place in that Northern California community every August.

- ◆ **Promoted by the Goodguys**
- ◆ **Open to cars up to 1972**
- ◆ **Other driving activities open to participants**

EMIL DIETRICH RACE CAR

The Emil Dietrich race car originally competed in the Modified Roadster class at SCTA speed trials on the Southern California dry lakes. A rule change in the late '40s put the car in the streamliner class, where it was outgunned by cars with more aerodynamically shaped bodies.

- ◆ **Set fastest speed at 1949 Bonneville Nationals**
- ◆ **Top speed was 154.53 mph**
- ◆ **Original paint**

Like many of the early modified racers that populated the dry lakes shortly before World War II, the Emil Dietrich car had to move to full streamline classification when new rules were instituted by the SCTA in the late '40s. The car was recently refurbished and preserved by Jim Lattin.

◆ **Single-seat racer**
◆ **Has all original running gear of pre-'50s era**
◆ **Made honorary pass to open 50th Bonneville Nationals**

'34 FORD

One thing about a late-model Chevrolet 350 small-block V-8: it's easy to make it look like one of the original 283s and 327s that GM offered during the early '60s. Don Mathis dressed his 350 with ribbed valve covers and Moon oil breathers. For really old-time effect, he topped the Chevy with an Offenhauser manifold and three Rochester 2G carbs.

◆ **The small-block came in many displacements**
◆ **Smallest is 265 cubic inches; largest 400 cubic inches**
◆ **By far the most popular engine for rodders**

NSRA NATIONALS

Street rods pack the parking lot at the NSRA Nationals (National Street Rod Association), looking like hundreds of colorful Easter eggs on a lawn. Between 10,000 and 13,000 street rods show up at Louisville, Kentucky, for the annual gathering, lending proof that rodding is as popular as ever.

◆ **First NSRA Nationals held in 1970 in Peoria, Illinois**
◆ **NSRA holds 10 regional Nationals**
◆ **Open to pre-'49 American cars only**